Bill Putnam taught for many years at Bournemouth University as Principal Lecturer in Archaeology. He has now retired, but continues to lecture widely to appreciative audiences on Dorset's archaeology. He spent eleven years digging the Roman villa at Dewlish, and seven exploring the Roman aqueduct at Dorchester. For twenty-three years he was Chairman of Wessex Archaeology, the major professional archaeological unit in the south-west of England. His other books include *Roman Dorset*, published by the Dovecote Press in 1984, of which this present book is a new revised edition for the 'Discover Dorset' series. As well as adding several new illustrations and being completely rewritten, 'Discover Dorset' *The Romans* incorporates the most recent research into the archaeology of Roman Dorset. Bill Putnam has also written *The Prehistoric Age* for the 'Discover Dorset' series, which tells the story of Dorset before the Romans came.

Following page
Alan Sorrell's reconstruction of the dramatic scene
as the Second Augusta Legion cuts its trunk road
(Ackling Dyke) across Iron Age Dorset.

DISCOVER DORSET

THE ROMANS

BILL PUTNAM

THE DOVECOTE PRESS

Mosaic detail, Frampton Roman villa.

First published in 2000 by The Dovecote Press Ltd
Stanbridge, Wimborne, Dorset BH21 4JD

ISBN 1 874336 74 1

© Bill Putnam 2000

Bill Putnam has asserted his rights under the Copyright, Designs
and Patent Act 1988 to be identified as author of this work

Series designed by Humphrey Stone

Typeset in Monotype Sabon
Printed and bound by Baskerville Press, Salisbury, Wiltshire

A CIP catalogue record for this book is available
from the British Library

3 5 7 9 8 6 4 2

CONTENTS

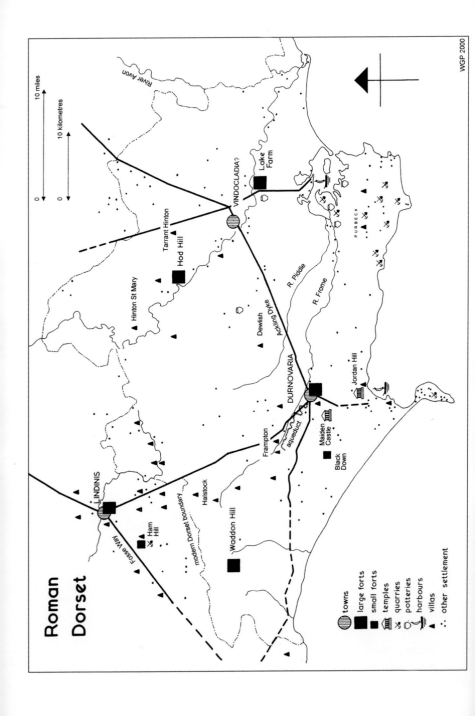

Roman
Dorset

WGP 2000

10 miles
0
10 kilometres
0

River AVON

VINDOCLADIA?
Lake Farm

Tarrant Hinton
Hod Hill

Hinton St Mary

Dewlish

Ackling Dyke

R. Piddle

R. Frome

PURBECK

Jordan Hill

DURNOVARIA

Frampton

aqueduct

Maiden Castle

Black Down

LINDINIS

Ham Hill

modern Dorset boundary

Halstock

Waddon Hill

Fosse Way

towns
large forts
small forts
temples
quarries
potteries
harbours
villas
other settlement

THE DUROTRIGES

Throughout the Iron Age and the Roman period Dorset was inhabited by a people called the Durotriges. Their territory was a little larger than modern Dorset. It extended to the Avon in the east, the Wylye in the north, and at least as far as the Axe in the west. The hillforts of Ham Hill and South Cadbury, both in Somerset, were certainly Durotrigian.

The Iron Age lasted from about 750 BC to 43 AD, and the Roman period from 43 AD to 410 AD.

The place we now call Dorchester was where the Durotriges built their Roman-style capital in the last quarter of the first century AD, but the significance of the area as a tribal centre may in fact go back a lot further, to Neolithic times. Maumbury Rings, later to become a Roman amphitheatre, began life as a Neolithic henge monument, similar to the earliest stage of Stonehenge. Mount Pleasant, on the eastern outskirts of the town was the site of another major henge, and in Greyhound Yard, Dorchester, a huge Neolithic circle or processional way was found, built of tree trunks let three metres into the ground.

It may seem surprising that we can put a name to the Durotriges at all. But though their early days were before history, once they came into contact with the Greek and Roman world – and this happened through trade long before the invasion of 43 AD – then written records became possible.

Even so, we are lucky to know their name; it only occurs in three places; on two building inscriptions put up by Durotrigian work parties on Hadrian's Wall, and in the *Geography* of Ptolemy, a Greek writing in Alexandria in about 50 AD. Ptolemy and one of the wall stones calls them Durotriges; the second wall stone (from Housesteads) calls them Durotrages. Durotrages must remain a possibility, but they are usually known as the Durotriges.

Since we know so little of them, how can we define their territory? There are two main ways of doing this; first by the location of finds of their characteristic dark brown or black burnished pottery, and secondly by finds of their own distinctive coins. These were silver staters and quarter-staters, and bronze staters, but unlike the tribes in south-eastern Britain, they had not taken to inscribing their king's names or names of their cities in Latin letters. As far as we know, they were illiterate. However, two apparently Durotrigian coins have been found, one in central Dorset and one near Portsmouth, with the letters CRAB on them. Unfortunately we do not know what this means.

In the last centuries before the Roman conquest, they were certainly engaged in trade with the continent, particularly the Armorican peninsular (Brittany). Coins of Armorican tribes are occasionally found in Dorset. Large quantities of continental pottery were imported through the trading centre in the promontory fort at Hengistbury Head, until Caesar's defeat of the Veneti in 56 BC put an end to it. The Durotriges may even have helped Armorica in their revolt against the Romans.

In origin the Durotriges were probably a mixture of the indigenous people of Dorset (themselves already a mixture) with new groups, arriving from Armorica and elsewhere on the continent. They came initially to trade, later to settle and intermarry with the locals. A similar process has gone on ever since!

Thus we have Durotrigian Dorset, a distinct tribal area, fiercely defended, with its own coinage entirely different to the coinage of the Belgic tribes to the east. The Durotriges had a successful pottery industry that was to rise to even greater heights under Roman control. Their kings and lesser chieftains lived in heavily defended hillforts, which had gone some way to becoming towns.

Their population was large and they were prospering. It must not be thought that they all lived in the hillforts; the whole countryside was a network of farms and villages, and the small rectangular fields of their farms covered much of the landscape, including many areas which we tend to think of as being cultivated for the first time since the Second World War.

But all said and done, they were still an Iron Age tribe, living in what most people today would find quite intolerable conditions, close

A building stone found on Hadrian's Wall, recording repairs done by a
work party of Durotriges from Ilchester.

to nature and often in fear of attack. This is illustrated by one of the
commonest features of Iron Age sites, the grain storage pit. Here the
harvest was stored; the tops were camouflaged, in the hope of saving
their food in time of danger.

In the early summer of 43 AD (not that they named the years in that
way!) horsemen galloped from farm to farm, warning of an impending
invasion that was to take more from them than their food supplies.
The value of what it brought to them is a matter of debate.

THE ROMAN CONQUEST

In 43 AD the Durotriges suffered one of the most frightening experiences ever to befall Dorset.

The Romans had for many years ruled over the tribes in Gaul and to some extent in Germany. In fact the Gauls regarded themselves as Roman by now, the great days of Vercingetorix's revolt against Caesar already beyond living memory.

But the Channel, part of the Roman 'Ocean' which surrounded their known world, lay between the Romans and the island of *Britannia*. Caesar had raided Britain in 55 BC, and returned in 54 to conquer the south-eastern part. But political and military pressures on the continent took him back to Rome and the British conquest did not survive, in contrast to Gaul, which became part of the Roman Empire.

For 97 years the tribes of Britain remained independent, though with increasing trade connections with the Roman world. Then in 43 AD another Roman ruler, the emperor Claudius, found it expedient to return to Britain and complete Caesar's conquest.

Many have wondered why he did it. In fact Claudius needed a military victory to gain the support of the soldiers on whom his power depended, and probably this was the main reason behind the invasion. A pretext occurred in the form of an appeal for Roman help from a British prince called Berikos, and the invasion began in early July.

THE INVASION

Claudius did not command in person, but appointed his best general, Aulus Plautius, to command the army and become the first governor of the new province. Four legions crossed the Channel. These were II Augusta, IX Hispana, XIV Gemina and XX Valeria. All were drawn from other provinces where they were not needed. A legion was between 5,000 and 6,000 strong, and since they would have been accompanied by a similar number of auxiliary troops (archers, slingers, light infantry and cavalry) the total size of the force was about 45,000.

They landed at Richborough in Kent, and by the end of the summer the Belgic group of tribes in south-east Britain, themselves a threat to the Durotriges, had all been defeated or had submitted to suit their own ends. Claudius came in person to ride triumphantly into their capital Colchester on an elephant.

We do not know the exact movements of the four legions, but later in the year a legion which was almost certainly Legio II Augusta was building a fortress at Chichester and setting up bases on the fringe of the territory of the Atrebates to the east, who were friendly to the Romans.

The Durotriges not surprisingly resisted grimly. They had had little contact with Rome and had not been involved in the political manoeuvrings of recent years. The Roman invaders represented a threat as fearsome as that presented to the British by the German armies in 1939.

The Romans planned, at least initially, a province formed from the more developed Belgic tribes of the south-east, but for military reasons the frontier was drawn along a line from Lincoln to Seaton in Devon, and we now know that frontier as the Fosse Way. Unfortunately for the Durotriges, their territory was within the frontier; in any case their heavily fortified hilltop towns could not be left untouched on the Romans' southern flank.

THE WAR AGAINST THE DUROTRIGES

The result was a bitter war of conquest fought over a period which may have been as long as ten years. An advanced base of Legio II Augusta was built at Lake Farm, on the banks of the Stour at Wimborne. Here excavations by Poole Museums along the line of the Wimborne bypass have shown a tantalising glimpse of the defences and the buildings of a substantial fortress. Geophysical surveys of the meadows by the river suggest that the fortress covered 12 hectares (about 29 acres). This is big enough for a full legion when camping briefly on the march, but with wooden barrack blocks and store

Foundation trenches of timber barrack blocks in the Roman fort at
Lake Farm, on the banks of the River Stour at Wimborne.

buildings as were seen in the excavation, two or three cohorts of the
legion is a more likely size for the force stationed here, together with
many store buildings.

The Lake Farm fortress is connected by a well authenticated Roman
road (see chapter 5) directly to the sea at Poole Harbour, where a
Roman large quern stone found in the mud gives a glimpse of supplies
and equipment coming ashore.

We can name the commander (*legatus legionis*) of Legio II Augusta
at the time of the invasion, something rarely possible in the story of
Roman Britain. He was Vespasian, later to become emperor, and a
very good one at that. His life is described in eulogistic terms by the
writer Suetonius, who says 'he went to Britain, where he fought thirty
battles, conquered two warlike tribes, and captured more than twenty
towns, besides the whole of the Isle of Wight'.

The Durotriges are not mentioned, but the Isle of Wight confirms
that he came in this direction and the twenty *oppida* he captured must
surely have been the great hillforts of the Durotriges. We are not
certain how long he stayed, but he was almost certainly responsible for

The Emperor Vespasian, seen here on a coin. Earlier in
his career, as commander of the Second Legion Augusta,
he was responsible for the invasion of Dorset.

the conquest of the Dorset. Several of the Durotrigian hillforts have
revealed traces of the violent assaults that occurred. Hundreds were
killed, and many may have been sold into slavery.

Undoubtedly the most spectacular evidence is provided by Hod Hill
near Blandford. Excavations by the British Museum in the 1950s
showed that one of the cohorts of Legio II Augusta, probably
accompanied by a regiment of cavalry, was stationed here in an
unusual fort built actually inside the native hillfort. It is visually the
most dramatic site in the whole of the conquest story.

Clearly the Durotrigian inhabitants were no longer there when the
Roman fort was built. They were dead, sold, or scattered in the
countryside waging guerilla warfare. The excavations found many
iron heads of ballista bolts, the mechanically fired arrows of the
legion's light artillery. Significantly a large group were concentrated in
one particular native hut which had its own enclosure within the
hillfort; it may well be that the barrage was concentrated on the
chieftain's hut.

The Roman occupation of Hod Hill lasted only for a short time,

Hod Hill near Blandford. The main outline is that of the Iron Age hillfort, and in the bottom part the streets and huts can be distinguished. In the top right hand corner lie the very different fortifications of the Roman fort inserted into it. This probably housed a cohort of the Second Legion Augusta and an auxiliary regiment of cavalry.

Buckle from a Roman soldier's belt, evidence of the
presence of the army in Dorchester.

during which it controlled the River Stour and protected Lake Farm.
This latter task was taken over by Waddon Hill near Beaminster in the
early fifties, protecting the new harbour at Weymouth, and the same
units may have been moved to Waddon. Neither Hod Hill nor
Waddon were on the permanent military road network, and their use
was short-lived.

Other such forts must have existed. Probably one has been quarried
away at Ham Hill, near Ilminster. Roman military buildings existed at
South Cadbury, but it is not clear how extensive they were. Similar
traces were found in Maiden Castle during the excavations of 1986.
Yet others may exist undetected or destroyed, and some smaller forts
are known.

By about 55 AD the legion had moved its headquarters from
Chichester to Exeter, and this may indicate the completion of the
conquest of the Durotriges.

DORCHESTER

Dorchester as a town did not exist at this time. It is certain that the
Roman army built a base somewhere near the site of the later town,
but exactly what and where provides one of the most tantalising
puzzles of the whole story.

All the Roman roads of Dorset were built by the army for their own
purposes. Dorchester is at a road junction near the crossing of the

The Iron Age hillfort of Maiden Castle near Dorchester. The east gate where the cemetery was found is to the right, and the foundations of the Roman temple can just be seen on the far side.

River Frome, and a fort must have been built to protect this important location. The roads as first laid out do not point directly at the later civilian town, but rather at the area of the Fairfield on the southern edge of Dorchester, and it may be that the fort was here. Excavation has not been possible to test this theory.

It is likely that the great hillfort of Maiden Castle had been of prime importance in Iron Age Dorset, and a fort to control the centre of Durotrigian authority would have been essential. A Roman bone sword handle was found on the site of the present Post Office, and a soldier's belt buckle was found on the Fairfield itself. Coins of

Claudian date have been found in various parts of Dorchester.

But the major indication that a Roman fort lay on the southern fringe of Dorchester is to be found in the Roman amphitheatre (Maumbury Rings) and the Roman aqueduct. Excavation in the amphitheatre has shown that it was built perhaps in the 50s AD, long before the town existed, and must therefore belong to the fort (all permanent or semi-permanent Roman forts had amphitheatres). Later, when the army had left Dorset, it became the town's amphitheatre.

Similarly the aqueduct which brought water from a stream near Frampton, north-west of Dorchester, has been shown to be a military aqueduct, originally supplying the Roman fort, and later diverted to the town. Both these features strongly suggest that the fort lay somewhere on or near the Fairfield.

There are two other artefacts which may be connected with the Roman fort, though their significance is uncertain. At Whitcombe, near Dorchester, a carved stone was found which may possibly be part of a cavalryman's tombstone. In the structure of the church at Godmanstone is a re-used altar stone dedicated to Jupiter Optimus Maximus by a centurion (though it appears to refer to a legion other than II Augusta).

MAIDEN CASTLE

Sir Mortimer Wheeler's excavations here in the 1930s, and more recent work in the 1980s, provide grim details about the Roman assault. The Durotrigians attempted in vain to defend their hillfort against an army which was trained and equipped to storm much more sophisticated defences than those of Maiden Castle.

It is likely that only one cohort of the legion would have been needed; certainly part of the legion was present, as at least one defender was killed by a ballista bolt from its artillery. No elaborate siege works were needed, or the traces would survive today; perhaps the legionaries formed a *testudo* ('tortoise' formation with shields locked over their heads) and approached the gates. They may have sawn through the bolts, or lit a fire to burn them, or battered them down with a ram. All the time volleys of ballista bolts swept the ramparts, killing those who rashly stood in view.

The cemetery in the eastern entrance to Maiden Castle, as uncovered by Sir Mortimer Wheeler in the 1930s.

It was one of these men whose body was found by Wheeler, the spine still dramatically pierced by the head of the bolt which killed him. He lay with 37 others, men and women, buried in the eastern entrance to the hillfort. Several others were apparently finished off with Roman weapons. Wheeler thought that they had all died in the battle, but now archaeologists regard the cemetery as one of the hillfort's regular features, and the manner of burial normal for the Iron Age people of the time. Certainly those killed in the battle were buried by their own people.

THE END OF THE CAMPAIGN

It is a mistake to imagine the Roman army patrolling Dorset throughout the three and a half centuries that Britain was part of the

Close up of a skeleton from the cemetery at Maiden Castle. Piercing one of the vertebrae is the iron head of a bolt fired from a legionary ballista, the most dramatic evidence imaginable of a Roman attack.

Roman empire. There is no evidence of any of the forts being occupied after about 65 AD, and even the legionary fortress at Exeter is abandoned soon after that, and Legio II Augusta moved eventually (in 75 AD) to its permanent home in Caerleon in South Wales.

By the late seventies the civilian towns were being built, and Romanisation was in full swing. Clearly by then the battle was won by the Romans, and Dorset was becoming fully integrated into the Roman world. The soldiers moved away to the north, where they remained permanently on guard.

But at least in the north of the territory of the Durotriges there is evidence at South Cadbury Castle of a last stand, which left its dead lying unburied in the south-west gateway. This may have been in 60 AD, when Boudica, Queen of the Iceni of Norfolk, led her people and many others in a final attempt to gain their freedom. All available Roman troops were dispatched to the Midlands, where under the command of Suetonius Paulinus they ultimately defeated Boudica.

We are told that the legion from the south-west did not arrive, and its commander committed suicide. Perhaps his soldiers were pinned down as they faced the last desperate rebellion by the Durotriges of Dorset and were unable to march north.

GOVERNMENT

THE CIVITAS

The Romans chose as their units of self government in Britain the native tribes as they existed before the invasion. Some had welcomed the Romans, and were rewarded with a special 'client King' status for their leaders. Among these were Cogidubnus in Sussex and Prasutagus in Norfolk. Others, which resisted strongly, were more harshly treated. But the privileged tribes lost their privileges when their original leader died, and all ended as normal *civitates* (counties) in the Roman province.

Each *civitas* had its capital, and in the case of the Durotriges (as we shall see in the next chapter) this was *Durnovaria*, or Dorchester. The *civitas* capitals were the lowest grade of town in the province. Above them came the *municipia*, towns rewarded by the grant of Latin Citizenship, an inferior form of Roman Citizenship. *Verulamium* is the only known example. Above them were the *coloniae*, cities actually formed from Roman citizens. The first of these was Colchester, no doubt populated by veterans of Claudius' invading army. Later came Lincoln, Gloucester and York.

CITIZENSHIP

The citizens of *Durnovaria* had to be content with citizenship of their own tribe, the Durotriges. Full Roman citizenship was something very much coveted, in view of the privileges it brought. St Paul was taken to Rome to a hearing before the emperor because of his citizenship. The only tombstone from *Durnovaria* records Carinus, 'Roman citizen'. The size of the letters indicates the importance of his citizenship.

There was one principal way of gaining Roman citizenship and that was by service in the army. The auxiliary regiments were formed from non-citizens, and after 25 years service the reward was citizenship for the soldier and for his wife and children. No doubt Durotrigians would have been among the British regiments found serving in various parts of the empire. However soon after 200 AD the emperor Caracalla granted citizenship to all those within the empire, and this distinction disappeared.

Not only were the inhabitants of Dorset citizens of their own *civitas*, but they were governed under native or Celtic law, not under Roman law. Celtic law was that of the native tribe as modified by the Roman government to match their own system. And on a capital charge a citizen had the right of appeal to the governor, in the same way as the Roman citizen could appeal to the emperor.

Everyday justice among the Durotriges was according to traditional Celtic law, and administered by Durotrigian judges. The governor went on circuit during the winter, when the armies were not campaigning, and no doubt from time to time the governor sat in judgement in *Durnovaria*. After the time of Agricola (77-84 AD) the appeal cases may well have been heard by the *legatus iuridicus*, a lawyer appointed to help the governor with his legal duties.

THE COUNCIL

The Durotriges were governed by a 'county' council, similar in functions to the modern one, but rather less democratic in its workings. This was called the *Ordo* or the 'order'. Its name and the names of its officers were similar to those of cities all over the Roman world.

Its members, theoretically a hundred but usually fewer, were *decuriones* or *decurions*. These were the elders and nobles of the Durotrigian tribe, retaining their position of privilege. Membership depended on a property qualification. They became. at least on the surface, more fully Romanised than the rest of the people. They owned the rich town houses with elaborate mosaic floors; many also owned a country house, or villa. Much of the trade and its profits were in their hands, as it had been before the conquest. We cannot, alas, put a name to a single one of them. The nearest we can really get to them is to admire the mosaics which graced their living room floors. For them the conquest meant a dramatic change in lifestyle, unlike the poorer people in the countryside.

The *ordo* made policy of its own accord in limited local areas of government, but more often interpreted centrally issued edicts of the governor or emperor. Perhaps in the last years of Roman Britain, as central government broke down, they came into their own, but we know little of this period.

THE MAGISTRATES

Their chief executives were known as *Duoviri Iuridicundo*. 'Duo' means two, and in accordance with Roman tradition of public office there were two of them, as of every other office. Either could veto the actions of the other. A curious system to our way of thinking, but designed to prevent abuse of office. For a similar reason the posts were annual. The *duovirs* administered local justice and presided at meetings of the *ordo* and the public assembly (*comitia*). They were responsible for public shows and the great religious festivals.

In addition there were two *aediles* or public works officers, who ran the roads, the drains, and the water supply, and looked after public buildings. Two *quaestors* may have looked after local finances, but most taxation was collected by contractors on behalf of central government. Every fifth year a senior pair of magistrates were chosen to conduct the census.

Theoretically all these magistrates were chosen by the people at the popular assembly in the market-place (or in Maumbury Rings?). But the *ordo* recommended candidates to the people, and as the years passed the people's view became less and less important.

The prestige of office was great, but so were the expenses. If successful, you paid the bill for the election, and were expected to provide public entertainment, or build a temple, or aqueduct or statue at your own expense. By the end of Roman Britain, citizens were reluctant to stand for office, and compulsion was introduced. Many decurions tried to move out of town to avoid it, something ultimately prohibited by decree.

THE PROVINCIAL COUNCIL

The *ordo* elected two representatives to the *concilium provinciae*, or provincial council, which met in London. At first sight this looks like a regional government advising the governor; but far from it. The governor was entirely autocratic and the provincial council met for formal purposes only, mainly connected with the Imperial Cult, the worship of the emperor.

THE GOVERNOR

The governor kept his eye on what happened in *Durnovaria* through his own large civil service in London. The flow of paperwork from Dorset to London rivalled that of today, but none of it survives. The top men in the civil service were all seconded soldiers from the legions. Many grades of officials existed. In particular the *speculatores* (inspectors) travelled the province as personal representatives of the governor, and will often have been in *Durnovaria*. All over the country you would have found *beneficiarii* or 'beneficiaries', who were in positions of trust, running post stations, organising taxes and otherwise representing the governor's interests.

TAXATION

The benefits, if such they were, of Roman life, had to be paid for. Every five years the census detailed people and property, and taxation was based on this. The *Procurator Augusti Britanniae* was responsible for the finances of the province, and under him other procurators had smaller areas of responsibility. One procurator of Britain, Classicianus, achieved fame by bringing to an end the slaughter following the rebellion of Boudica. (The procurator had a direct line of communication to the emperor.)

The Durotriges paid the three standard taxes to the tax contractors: the *annona*, or corn tax, to feed the army, the *tributum soli*, based on the productivity of the land, and the *tributum capitis* or poll tax. No doubt they paid up, reluctantly.

THE TOWNS

DORCHESTER

Dorchester was called *Durnovaria* by the Romans. We are lucky to know this as it occurs in only one ancient document, the Antonine Itinerary (a third century route book). Most versions of the book actually spell it *Durnonovaria*, but one has *Durnovaria* and this is the name hallowed by use in modern times. No one is sure what it means, except that the first part may refer to fist-sized pebbles.

The gates and many public buildings must have carried monumental inscriptions recording the name and other valuable information but alas, not one has survived; the only inscriptions are on an altar dedicated by a legionary centurion (in Godmanstone church), a tombstone (see below) and a stamped tile. None of these name the town or the tribe.

The nearness of Maiden Castle and the later history of the town strongly suggest that Dorchester was the Roman capital of the Durotriges; but surprisingly this cannot be proved beyond doubt. Nowhere in the Antonine Itinerary is the name of the tribe attached to the name of the town – *Durnovaria Durotrigum* – as was normally done with tribal capitals.

ROMANISATION

The Romans were very good at persuading conquered tribes to accept the Roman way of life and to acquiesce in Roman rule. It was more profitable than indefinite military control. One of the ways in which this was done was by retaining the nominal 'independence' of the local tribe and gaining the support of their leaders through formal recognition of their position and other benefits. Once possessed of beautiful villas, steam baths and the other trappings of Roman civilisation, the princes of the Durotriges were scarcely likely to lead a

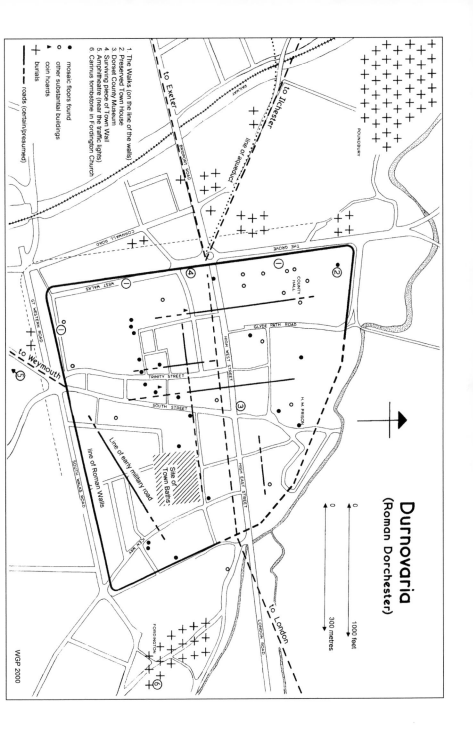

Durnovaria
(Roman Dorchester)

1. The Walks (on the line of the walls)
2. Preserved Town House
3. Dorset County Museum
4. Surviving piece of Town Wall
5. Amphitheatre (near the traffic lights)
6. Carinus tombstone in Fordington Church

● mosaic floors found
○ other substantial buildings
▲ coin hoards
+ burials
▬ ▬ roads (certain/presumed)

0   1000 feet
0   300 metres

WGP 2000

to Exeter
to Ilchester
to Weymouth
to London

RAILWAY
line of aqueduct
POUNDBURY
BRIDPORT ROAD
CORNWALL ROAD
THE GROVE
GT WESTERN ROAD
WEST WALKS
COUNTY HALL
GLYDE PATH ROAD
HIGH WEST STREET
TRINITY STREET
SOUTH STREET
H. M. PRISON
HIGH EAST STREET
SOUTH WALKS ROAD
Site of Town Baths
Line of early military road
Line of Roman Walls
ICEN WAY
FORDINGTON
LONDON ROAD

movement advocating a rebellious return to the windswept hilltop of Maiden Castle. It has even been suggested that the famous and magnificent Roman palace of Fishbourne, near Chichester, represents a direct reward to Cogidubnus, the pro-Roman chief of the Regnenses, and was used to entice the leaders of other tribes into Roman ways.

By and large, throughout the new province of *Britannia*, the Romans used the existing tribal groupings as the basis of their administrative divisions. Thus the Durotriges were made into a *civitas*. This is a word best left in Latin, as it means both the 'county' in geographical terms and the people themselves – a sort of 'county state'.

A *civitas* needed a *civitas* capital, and this was to be Dorchester. All over Britain tribal governments were moved from the draughty hillforts (or wherever they had been moved to since the invasion) down to lower ground, usually taking over now disused army camps to provide their first temporary buildings; something like this happened at Dorchester, though the original army camp has not been identified.

When did this occur? We know the general answer to this question: in his life of Agricola, governor of Britain from 77 to 84 AD, Tacitus writes that he encouraged the building of temples, markets and houses. Those towns with firm evidence for their beginnings, such as Cirencester, confirm that this was so. No doubt Dorchester was similar, though the evidence is not yet conclusive.

The governor may have appointed a *praefectus civitatis*, or civitas prefect, whose job was to advise the Durotrigian princes on the setting up of a Roman style town as their capital, and a system of government in line with that of Roman towns throughout the empire..

No name can be put to a *praefectus civitatis* in Britain, but it is tempting to think that Carinus, whose tombstone records his Roman citizenship so proudly at an early date in the history of Dorchester, could originally have arrived as the prefect and stayed to settle.

Though the governor provided encouragement and technical assistance (and no doubt compulsion if needed) the Durotriges had to pay for their own city. The Roman writer and philosopher Seneca is known to have lent millions of sesterces to British tribes to fund their Romanisation programme.

The building of Dorchester must have been a financial strain. We do not know how soon elaborate and expensive public buildings appeared. The wealthy buildings we know of belong to the later third and the fourth century, but they must have had their timber predecessors in the first and second centuries.

Excavations in Dorchester in the last fifty years have made one thing very clear; the builders of Saxon and medieval Dorchester used the Roman buildings as a quarry on a systematic and, for the archaeologist, devastating scale. Time and time again all the archaeologists find of Roman buildings are the empty foundation trenches. Not only has all the dressed stone and brick from the walls gone, but the foundations have been quarried away to the last flint.

In these circumstances it is difficult to offer reliable opinions on the appearance of the town at various stages of its Roman history, and particular importance attaches to the rare sites where substantial parts of Roman buildings have been found. These include the very well preserved town house behind County Hall, and the sequence of buildings found at 34 Trinity Street; these ranged from simple timber buildings in the first century, timber framed buildings on stone foundations in the second, to a substantial stone and flint town house in the fourth.

DURNOVARIA

THE WALLS. Like most Roman towns in Britain the town was walled. The outline of the walls can clearly be seen from the air. Walls and ditches covered a swathe over 100 metres wide. This has dominated the pattern of the town till Victorian times; not till then did the town spread outside.

The walls are best understood in the south-west corner in Bowling Alley Walk. The wall stood on the edge of the grass verge. The bank which backed the wall (and contained the chalk from the ditches) extends across the path and some 20 metres into the former hospital grounds. The triple ditches extended further south, the outer, southernmost, one being under the far side of Great Western Road. Beyond that still, lay the counterscarp bank, under the houses on the south of the road. The scale of the work was enormous.

The ruined walls were cleared and the Walks constructed in the early eighteenth century, fortunately for us making a permanent marker of their route. Their position is clear on the west, south and southern part of the east side. Only on the north is their route uncertain, where the building of the castle and later the prison, and possible erosion by the river, has made it impossible to know what happened.

At a point just south of the Top o' Town roundabout a fragment of walling survives. The facing stones have long since disappeared, but the core shows traces of the Roman style of building, with levelling courses of horizontal stones at intervals.

Imposing gates must have existed, on the west, south and east sides, but no trace has ever been found. Their positions can be calculated from the lines of the roads within the town, which are known in part from excavation. The streets do not by any means correspond with the modern ones.

At first the towns, with one or two exceptions, did not have walls. Under the Roman peace (*pax Romana*) such things were unnecessary. Citizens were not allowed to carry arms. But in 196 AD, the governor Clodius Albinus did something later imitated by other governors of Britain. He declared himself Augustus and took the British legions to the continent to make himself emperor. Before he went, he took steps to make it possible for the province to survive attack in his absence. The essential feature of Roman life and control was the towns, and he gave orders for them to be walled to protect themselves. The walls enclosed the areas that had already been built upon, in the case of Dorchester about 30 hectares (75 acres). This is the reason for the irregular shape of the town.

An interesting discovery in excavations on the walls in Bowling Alley Walk was that prior to the erection of the earliest earth and timber rampart a start had been made on the foundations of a stone wall. This had got no further, when the presumably urgent construction of a massive (but quicker) earth bank buried it.

The walls did not finally gain a stone face till some time in the third century. (The date for this is very uncertain, and the date for the original construction is not beyond doubt.) Many towns acquired bastions for artillery on the outer face of the walls in the fourth century. This may have happened at Dorchester, but there is no evidence for it.

A view of the 1977 excavation of the public baths of Roman Dorchester. Parts of several suites of heated rooms are visible, and prominent in the centre is a large *laconicum* or sauna.

PUBLIC BUILDINGS. Nothing is known of the *forum* (market-place) and *basilica* (town hall), though some indication of its position near Cornhill can be gained from the plan of the internal roads of the town.

The *thermae* or heated baths were partly excavated by the Central Excavation Unit of the Department of the Environment in 1977. They lay in the south-east quarter under the former rugby pitch of Hardye's Junior School at Wollaston House. After excavation they were reburied, and cannot be seen today.

The baths form the most substantial masonry remains of Roman buildings so far found in Dorchester. Though robbing of the stone had been extensive, the massive scale of the building ensured that parts of hypocausts and water tanks survived. It is clear that the building covered an area at least 100 metres by 150 metres and must have been most impressive. It included several suites of the usual series of cold, tepid and hot rooms, and a large *palaestra* (exercise yard) to the north.

The baths would have been one of the main social centres of the town and it is an indication of the depth of Romanisation that such a very Roman feature should have flourished in this remote corner of the Roman empire.

An aerial photograph of the Roman amphitheatre at Dorchester, Maumbury Rings. The amphitheatre was originally built for the Roman fort, which must lie close by.

MAUMBURY RINGS. Outside the town on the road to the harbour at Weymouth, lay the amphitheatre. Maumbury Rings is a far cry from the Colosseum in Rome, but its function was basically similar. We have already seen how it had a military use at first, but certainly it was adapted to use for the town at an early date.

It was entirely built of earth and timber, and never rebuilt in stone. Perhaps Dorchester would never have had an amphitheatre had the military one not been to hand; certainly it was no longer used by the mid-second century. Whether Christians were fed to the lions there, or gladiators fell in combat, is doubtful. Such shows were expensive to put on, and *Durnovaria* is unlikely to have supported them. But some form of entertainment must have occurred there, no doubt reminiscent of the modern circus. Perhaps these were a financial disaster, and this lead to the abandonment.

THE AQUEDUCT.   There is one feature of Roman towns where Dorchester has the best example in the whole of Britain. This is the water supply aqueduct. A constant supply of fresh, clean water was essential to a Roman town. The public baths used enormous quantities and filling their various pools and boilers from a well by buckets would have been tedious though not impossible. Nevertheless the town had wells, and so would always have had drinking water available.

In and around Rome itself some 11 water channels brought water to the city from the surrounding hills on overhead masonry structures. Nothing as impressive (and expensive) as this existed at Dorchester. A single channel collected water from a tributary of the Frome at Frampton, and by keeping to a minimum gradient just managed to deliver it at ground level at the West gate.

It followed the contours, rather than cross low ground on masonry structures, and thus followed a very devious path. It can be seen at its best in Fordington Bottom, where a channel is still open at apparent dimensions of about 3 metres wide and 1.5 metres deep. But excavations have shown that this is misleading. The actual channel

Students of Bournemouth University at work on the excavations
of the Dorchester Roman aqueduct.

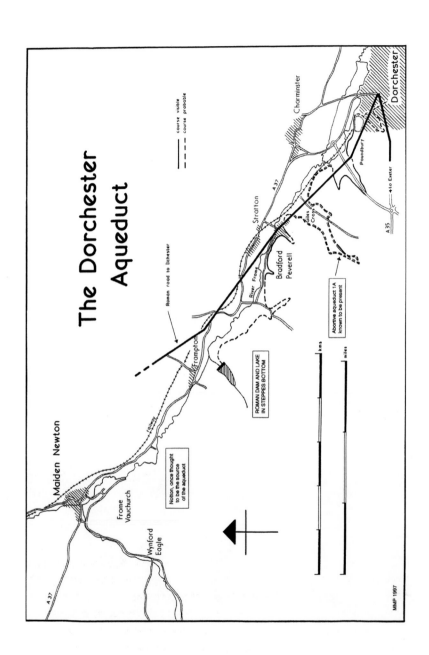

The Dorchester Aqueduct

course visible
course probable

Maiden Newton

Frome Vauchurch

Wynford Eagle

A 37

Notton, once thought to be the source of the aqueduct

Compton

Colway

Roman road to Ilchester

River Frome

Bradford Peverell

Stratton

A 37

ROMAN DAM AND LAKE IN STEPPES BOTTOM

Abortive aqueduct 1 A known to be present

Miles Cross

Poundbury

Charminster

Dorchester

A 35

to Exeter

kms

miles

MMP 1997

[32]

was 80 centimetres wide by 30 centimetres deep, made of wood and clay, and buried out of sight. What can be seen in Fordington Bottom is an attempt at reconstruction which was abandoned when the old aqueduct had been dug out – what you see is a construction trench.

At its source there was a dam. Excavations in 1997-8 located this at Littlewood Farm, Frampton, and this is where the 9 mile aqueduct started its journey. Beside the dam lies a small Roman fort. The only possible reason for a fort in such a location is to provide protection for the builders of the aqueduct, and thus it is clear the Roman army provided the expertise. They originally built it for the military fort at Dorchester, and it was later adapted to serve the new town.

Once the town was built the aqueduct must have delivered its water to the *castellum aquae,* or public fountain, about half way down Princes Street. At the fountain the street mains began, and users like the baths would have had their own inlet; charges were based on the size of the inlet. One timber water main has been located running along Princes Street and Durngate Street towards the baths; the wooden pipes have rotted, but the iron collars which joined the lengths survive.

By about 160 AD the aqueduct was out of use, like the amphitheatre. From that time water will have come from wells, and it seems that even the baths will have had to manage that way.

THE HOUSES. Roman towns, like modern ones, contained an enormous variety of houses and other buildings. The *decurions* (see page 21) would have town houses of considerable splendour, with elaborate dining rooms, mosaic floors, formal gardens, and their own suite of baths. One of these was found in 1937 during excavations prior to the building of County Hall, and its remains have now been reconsolidated and placed in view under an impressive roof built in the Roman style of the original.

There will have been many others, and some have been glimpsed at various times and their mosaic pavements lifted or reburied (two have been installed in the floor of Dorset County Museum). Other houses will have been smaller and poorer, and many artisans will have lived over their shops in crowded streets. But none of these have been excavated to date.

The mosaic floor discovered in 1899 in Olga Road, Dorchester. It is now
set into the floor of the Victorian gallery of Dorset County Museum.

In the fringes of the town small scale industries existed (most
Roman industries were small scale), and some of their workshops and
furnaces have been seen on the County Hall site and under the old
Hospital. None of these are now on view.

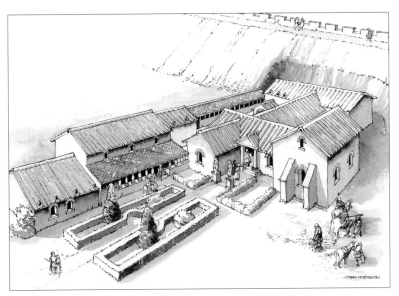

An imaginative reconstruction by John Hodgson of the Roman Town House in Colliton Park, Dorchester, as it might have looked in the 4th century AD.

Excavations in 1937 on the Roman town house in Colliton Park. This has been partially reconstructed and is on view to the public.

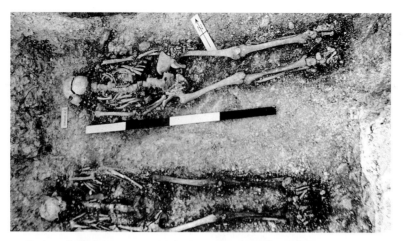

Rows of Christian graves in the Poundbury Roman cemetery outside Dorchester. The site is now occupied by an industrial estate.

THE CEMETERIES.   Around Durnovaria stretched the cemeteries, originally along the roads but later filling in considerable areas between them. Two areas have been extensively excavated; the Poundbury industrial estate, and Fordington High Street. At Poundbury excavations by Christopher Sparey Green over a number of years revealed over 1,000 graves, their occupants rescued from the bulldozers constructing the industrial estate. A majority belonged to the fourth century AD, a time when the Roman empire was officially Christian. They were buried on an east-west alignment and for the most part without grave goods. Family groups were in stone *mausolea* with paintings on the walls. Fragments of these give a tantalising clues to the Christian ritual of the cemetery.

Most of the bodies were in wooden coffins, but the more important ones had lead linings, and a few were in hamstone coffins. Such coffins provide important evidence, as even hair may survive in such conditions. The bones from Poundbury have been analysed and published, and give a substantial sample of the people of *Durnovaria* in the fourth century, with details of their size, appearance, diseases, and the other information which can now be obtained from such remains.

In Fordington most burials were excavated in Victorian times

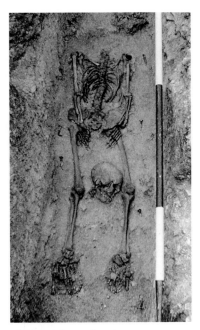

A bizarre Roman skeleton from the pagan cemetery at Fordington. The woman's head has been removed and buried between her knees. There must be a reason of a religious or magical nature.

though there have been small excavations recently. Much of the village was covered by the cemetery. Here there was a greater variety of burial, ranging from the Christian to flexed burials which, though dating to the fourth century, reflected the burial pattern of the native Durotriges. There were also cremations, common in the Roman world in the first two centuries AD.

Most interesting of all is the one and only inscribed tombstone to be found, re-used in the porch of St George's, Fordington. This stone, found in 1907, can still be seen in the church at the west end, and there is a replica in Dorset County Museum. It is made of Purbeck marble, and would have been set in an ornamental surround, and brightly painted. It is the only tombstone surviving; there can hardly have been a large number, unless the cemeteries were stripped of the stones (as in London) to provide emergency building materials in the last years of Roman Britain. The stone belongs to the early years of the town, and

The tombstone of Carinus, Fordington.

must represent someone important. Unfortunately no indication is given of his function. The stone reads:

CARINO
CIVI.ROM
ANN.L
RUFINUS.ET
CARINA.ET
AVITA.FILI.EIUS
ET.ROMANA.UXOR

('In memory of) Carinus, Roman citizen, (died) aged 50 years. His children, Rufinus, Carina and Avita, with his wife Romana, (set up this memorial').

So we can put a name to these five inhabitants of earliest Dorchester. Clearly Carinus' Roman citizenship was of the greatest importance. There would not have been many such in *Durnovaria* in the first and second centuries. Maybe he was a citizen from elsewhere in the empire who came on government business, came to love Dorset and stayed. He can hardly have been a Durotrigian native, as his name is not appropriate.

ILCHESTER   There is a second town in Durotrigian territory, namely Ilchester (*Lindinis*). Its name appears on two inscribed construction stones from Hadrian's Wall, recording the work of a construction gang provided by the Durotriges. The inscriptions read (in an abbreviated form):

C DUROTRIGUM LINDINIESIS

This means the '*civitas* of the Durotriges from *Lindinis*'. It might mean that Ilchester became a separate *civitas*, but more likely this stone was erected by the Ilchester gang, while another (lost) stone recorded the work of the Dorchester gang.

Lindinis was smaller than *Durnovaria*, some 12 hectares (30 acres) in extent. We know even less about it, though excavations in recent years have begun to tell its story, a story which is complicated and not yet understood. Today, of course, it is in Somerset, but it was certainly part of Dorset to its ancient inhabitants. Ilchester was on the early Roman frontier, the Fosse Way. It is not surprising, therefore, to find it was also originally a Roman fort site. The defences of one fort have been located under the town, while at least one other exists outside the town to the north-east. At Ilchester the Fosse Way crossed the River Yeo, and this is the kind of site to be guarded by a fort.

As in Dorchester, chance finds and excavations alike have produced indications of rich men's houses and other poorer buildings. Again the period of greatest prosperity seems to have been in the late third and fourth centuries.

OTHER SITES. Dorchester and Ilchester alone are walled towns laid out in a formal grid of streets. Other settlements existed (see page 51) and the settlement at Shapwick (near Badbury Rings) with an extraordinary fortified citadel was of considerable size. It was probably called *Vindocladia*.

Wareham is a town where substantial finds of Roman pottery have been made, particularly in the north-west and south-east quarters. It is tempting to imagine a small town representing the trading headquarters of the various Roman industries of Purbeck, and it may have been so. But the evidence is slight, the walls were certainly built by King Alfred, and there is no certain Roman road to connect it even to Dorchester.

ROADS

Think of the Romans, and their roads come first to mind. The Romans did not invent roads, as many of the preceding civilisations in the Middle East had them, but it was the Romans who developed them into the comprehensive system on which the administration of their empire depended. Naturally the system penetrated to Dorset.

Before the Romans came to Britain there were no roads at all, at least in the meaning of an engineered route with hard surface, foundations, drainage and bridges. There were trackways resulting from the passage of travellers; these trackways followed natural routes, and some of them, particularly the ridgeways, went for many miles. In some cases it seems that the Romans built roads which more or less followed the routes of these trackways.

The roads were one of the most drastic landscape changes that the Romans brought. All previous landscape features, even if man-made, were largely controlled by the presence of forests, rivers and hills. Now the route from A to B was in all probability a straight line drawn by an engineer on a map, and surveyed and carried out on the ground, initially at least, by the army. If your house unfortunately lay in its path, no planning permission or compulsory purchase order was needed for its destruction. Initially all the roads were built for military purposes; later they were adapted for the use of the new *civitates* and perhaps some new ones specially built.

CONSTRUCTION

Roman roads were straight except where the terrain prevented it; if necessary they zig-zagged on steep descents and even performed long gentle curves. Although visitors to Rome admire the *Via Appia*, constructed of lava blocks, and other similar paved roads, it must be remembered that the money for this sort of thing was rarely, if ever, available in Britain. British roads were of gravel (*via glareae* in Latin). There are just one or two possible cases of a paved road, and even these are doubtful.

Fine gravel as a running surface lay over larger stones forming a foundation. At each side lay a drainage ditch, and the road itself was normally carried on a causeway which can in some cases be surprisingly high (particularly Ackling Dyke); nevertheless the reason was the same, namely drainage. Nothing destroys a road faster than lying water and frost. In hollows, culverts carried surface water or streams beneath the road.

The roads were surprisingly narrow; although the causeway (or *agger*) may have been as much as 20 metres in width, the running surface at its top was rarely more than 3 metres wide. This was just enough for two vehicles moving slowly to pass. When traffic ruts survive, they are normally central on the road. Once a road has been ploughed over it gives the appearance of having been much wider; but this is unlikely to have been so.

Where streams were substantial, bridges were built, sometimes of stone, sometimes of timber. But if the stream was unlikely to hinder traffic, then a ford was often enough. No Roman bridge survives in Britain, in spite of many traditions that they do. Normally rivers have eaten away even the foundations, and roads usually disappear as they enter a river's flood plain

NAMES AND MILESTONES

Roman roads carried names, and usually commemorated the name of the consul or emperor under whom construction or repair was carried out. However, we do not know the Latin names for any of the Roman roads in Britain.

One milestone survives in Dorset. This was found in Dorchester during excavations on a building site. Unfortunately it was not in its original position, so we do not know which road it belonged to. The inscription reads:

IMP

POSTVMO

AUGG

The Roman milestone from Alington Avenue, Dorchester.

In full this was *Imperatori Postumo Augusto* '(in honour of) the emperor Postumus Augustus'. He lived in the third century AD, so the milestone probably refers to repairs to a road, rather than its original building.

An uninscribed stone outside Dorchester at the Stinsford roundabout might just be another very worn example.

Responsibility for maintenance of the roads, which initially was carried out by the army, was transferred to the local communities as soon as possible.

ROADS IN DORSET

Three routes are known for certain in Dorset. All were built by the Second Augustan Legion during the conquest. Some others have been claimed, but there is no firm proof for their existence. There may well have been minor routes, particularly to the industries of Purbeck, but these are not likely to have been constructed in the grand manner of Ackling Dyke, and very little trace survives.

Ackling Dyke, the Roman trunk road through Dorset, at Badbury Rings. Three Roman roads are visible: the original route to the Lake Farm fort and Poole harbour runs up the left hand side. The extension to the fort at Dorchester and Weymouth harbour crosses from low left to top right, and in the field in the foreground it is crossed by the later road towards Bath.

ACKLING DYKE (OLD SARUM – BADBURY – DORCHESTER – EXETER). The main road of Roman Dorset. Ultimately it came from London, via Staines, Silchester (near Reading) and Old Sarum (near Salisbury). The road passes through Dorset en route to Exeter. From about 55 AD till the late 60s the Second Augustan Legion had its headquarters at Exeter (*Isca*), and Ackling Dyke was its trunk road to London.

When first built it ran via Badbury Rings to the fortress at Lake Farm, Wimborne, and thence to Poole harbour. In its second stage a junction was put in at Badbury Rings and it was extended to Dorchester and Weymouth harbour. This section has been found passing at an angle beneath the later town of *Durnovaria*. In its third stage a junction was made near Dorchester, and the road extended, first to Seaton, and then to Exeter.

From Dorchester the road climbs soon after it leaves the town onto a ridge where it may have followed a prehistoric route. There are many short changes of direction. Near Eggardon Hillfort the road leaves the chalk high ground and drops onto the greensand, with its many small hills and valleys.

Here its route must have been tortuous, and tracing it is very difficult. There is sufficient evidence to suggest that it passed through or near to Bridport, Chideock, Morecombe Lake, Charmouth and Pen Cross, before leaving Dorset at Raymond's Hill. Its route does not become entirely clear again till it reaches Axminster.

Excavations on Roman roads tend to produce very little information, Two excavations have been carried out on Ackling Dyke, at points where it is in perfect condition, giving an indication of what it was like when it was built. In Thorncombe Wood (SY 727920) the road is on sand and gravel, and its *agger* is built of gravel dug from pits close to the road. The causeway is 8 metres wide at the base, narrowing at the top to a little over 3 metres (10ft). Central ruts were still visible on the surface. At Eggardon (SY 544937) the road was of similar dimensions, though the materials were entirely different. Here it lies on the chalk, and the causeway is of flint, quarried from the chalk nearby. The sloping sides were of chalk rubble (also from the quarries) but the running surface was of gravel clearly brought from some distance away, perhaps on Black Down near Portesham.

BADBURY RINGS – BATH. From the complex road junction at Badbury Rings the road ran across country in the direction of Bath. It is difficult to follow once it leaves Dorset and the chalk near Ashmore (ST 922175), but it is heading for the Bath area and perhaps the early Roman harbour at Sea Mills. It is tempting to visualise heavy equipment from Lake Farm moving towards the Bristol Channel from here as the campaigning area moved farther north.

DORCHESTER – ILCHESTER. Three miles from Dorchester the road crosses the Frome Valley between Bradford Peverell and Stratton (the name indicates the presence of a 'street'). From here the road turned to a more northerly direction, and for the most part lies under the modern A37. It can however be seen following an independent route at Hyde House (near Frampton), at Holywell (near Evershot) and just to the east of Melbury Park. It leaves Dorset near Ryme Intrinseca.

THE VILLAS

The main sign of Romanisation in the Dorset countryside was the appearance of villas. There is not much evidence for them in the first and second centuries AD, but in the third and fourth they began to be built in greater numbers, and towards the end of Roman rule in Britain some were both large and luxurious.

The Latin word *villa* means farm and implies that it is a substantial establishment with a farmhouse built to a considerable degree of luxury. Some of the villas near Rome itself were little short of palaces. While in smaller ones the farmyard was right in front of the house, in the larger villas farming activities were carried out round the back, and the main courtyard became a formal garden.

In Dorset, many of them represented the country homes of the native Durotrigian nobility, who would also have had a luxury house in town. The wealth needed to build them came from farming, from ownership of land, and from whatever industries the nobility had their money invested in.

The wealth shown by the villas in the fourth century would seem to imply that the Durotriges, or at least their leaders, had become very prosperous by then. It is a little difficult to see where this prosperity came from, and because of this some historians have suggested that the explanation lies in the arrival of men and their money from Gaul. Britain, particularly the west, may have seemed a haven from political troubles and Saxon attacks, and rich nobles of the tribes in Gaul may have bought up modest Durotrigian villas with their land, and modernised them. This is certainly a possible explanation, but at present, there is not enough evidence to decide.

The villas in Durotrigian territory are in two main groups; those around Ilchester (numerous, but mostly in Somerset now) and those around Dorchester. It is unusual to find large villas more than an hour or so on horseback from a town, but there were a few, such as Tarrant

A reconstruction by Peter Woodward of the landscape around the Dewlish Roman Villa in the 4th century AD (see page 51)

Hinton. These may have had special functions, such as the home of a procurator in charge of an imperial estate of some sort.

The villas of Dorset have suffered much damage over the centuries. Most were abandoned by their owners around 400 AD when growing economic and political chaos made it impossible to maintain them. Danger of attack (a possibility in Dorset, though a near certainty in many eastern parts of the province) persuaded owners to live in town and probably to transport their harvest there as soon as possible. Dorchester and Ilchester at least had walls to defend them.

The villas then suffered what every abandoned house suffers, ranging from small boys with catapults breaking the windows, to large scale digging in medieval times to find dressed stone to use in a new church. Often little but the mosaic floors survives; the floors are useless for building material, unless of course they lie over a hypocaust, or underfloor heating system. In such cases they may well have been torn up to get at the large slabs which carried them over the heating channels.

In the end the villas became slight bumps in the ground.

Nevertheless, the discovery of a mosaic floor belonging to a ruined villa still provides one of the most exciting moments in archaeology as the pictures and patterns of a bygone age are uncovered.

FRAMPTON

In the water meadows beside the Frome at Frampton lies one of the earliest villas to be discovered in Dorset. Found in 1796, its mosaic floors were cleared and drawn by Lysons. Its main interest lies in the Christian symbol, found in the floor pattern (see the illustration on the front cover). The floor was almost certainly laid in the fourth century. Almost nothing else is known about the house and its farm. Today there is nothing to see but an area of rubble surrounded by the artificial channels of the water meadows, which will have severely damaged the remaining parts of the villa. It is doubtful whether the pavements still survive under the soil.

Frampton is in fact a puzzle. Its site is on the flood plain of the River Frome, subject to flooding and of doubtful suitability for farming. It may be a religious site dedicated to a water god, though on the other hand its main room looks entirely appropriate as the *triclinium* (dining room) of a normal villa.

HINTON ST MARY

Hinton St Mary is the most famous of the Dorset villas. It was discovered by accident in 1963 when the village blacksmith was digging a hole for his wife's washing line! Oddly enough the villa suffered a similar fate to Frampton; we now know little more about it than can be deduced from the mosaic. This time the reason was the enormous publicity which followed the discovery, making further archaeological research difficult.

The publicity came from the fact that the mosaic floor had at its centre a picture of the head and shoulders of Christ. This is discussed in the chapter on Religion (see page 58). The floor was bought by the British Museum, and formed a major exhibit in its Romano-British display. More recently however it has been in store. As at Frampton, there is nothing to see at the site today.

Spectacular mosaics have not survived here, and the villa lies in close proximity to a considerable area of Romano-British settlement. It may not be the same sort of country house as the other villas described here. Its most spectacular finds have been a twin-cylinder pump from its well, and an inscription on a sandstone block, also thrown down into the well. The inscription is important, as inscriptions from villas are very rare indeed. It is a tombstone from the cemetery belonging to the villa or the settlement. It reads:

CUP VEP DECESSIT ANNO XXXVIIII TUSCO
ET BASSO COS VII KAL SEPTEMB

(Cupitius Vep . . . died in his 39th year in the consulship of Tuscus and Bassus, on the 26th August.)

Mentioning the names of the consuls is a common method of naming the year, in this case 258 AD. Although the inscription mentions September, the date is actually in August, because Roman dates are given as so many days before certain fixed points in the month (in this case seven days, counting inclusively, before the 1st of September).

Most interesting of all is the second name, beginning with Vep . . . It may be that it is Celtic rather than Roman. Thus it is possible that Vep . . . is the only Romano-British Durotrigian native to whom we can put a name, or at least part of one! He could, however, have come from any other Celtic tribe.

The pump is of great interest. Made of a wooden block, with bronze and lead working parts, it may have been worked by slaves or a treadmill to pump water from the well. Such items of engineering were common enough in the Roman world, but their survival is rare.

HALSTOCK

At Halstock a very large courtyard villa (of the group attached to Ilchester) has been fully excavated. The excavations, in difficult conditions on a wet clay soil, have produced spectacular baths, and some of the barns and other farm buildings. The main courtyard house has sadly been ploughed well below the level of its floors so that knowledge of large parts of the villa is confined to the ground plan given by the foundations. The villa has been fully published (see Further Reading).

DEWLISH

The site in the grounds of Dewlish House has a complex history. The dry summer of 1976 revealed many features in parch-marks in the grass. The earliest occupation was a very wide scatter of Mesolithic flints dating to about 6,000 BC. There is a farm of Iron Age date (not excavated) with its many grain storage pits and field enclosures. This was followed by small square 'Celtic' fields of the early part of the Roman period; but no trace of the farm of this date was found, and it is impossible to say whether it was a villa.

Then in the late third century AD the field banks were levelled and a small farm was built, just about qualifying as a villa. A single long building housed the owner at one end and the barn at the other. There were no mosaics, but the walls were plastered and painted.

Early in the fourth century these early buildings were converted entirely into enlarged farm buildings, and a larger luxury house was built on a second side of the courtyard, with a full length veranda and central porch. But still the floors were wooden or *opus signinum* (crushed brick concrete).

After a short life the villa was abandoned and allowed to fall down in part. Whether the same fate befell the farm is not clear, but it is unlikely. Then in the second half of the fourth century either prosperity returned or, more likely, the property was bought for renovation. The house was rebuilt, in some parts from the foundations up. The farm buildings were cleared away entirely, and in their place appeared a small temple and priest's house. The villa had become a small pagan religious settlement. The baths were enlarged - perhaps healing was a central feature of the cult - and almost every room in the main building was fitted with mosaic floors. At the back a large kitchen block was built, presumably to cope with the visitors.

Success did not last long; by about 400 AD the building was in ruins again, although the farming no doubt continued. But the farm buildings associated with the grand phase of the villa were clearly on

Dewlish Roman Villa; the moment of discovery of the mosaic
floor of the triclinium (dining room).

another site and have not been found. How far the history of Dewlish
villa is typical, remains to be seen.

The house was well preserved in places. Some of the mosaics were
reburied, some vulnerable fragments were taken up by Dorset County
Museum. The leopard and gazelle fragment hangs in Dewlish House.
Fragments of two successive floors of the baths changing room are in
Dorset County Museum. These show an interesting change of fashion
in floor patterns, from abstract geometric patterns, to a frieze of
fantastic sea creatures swimming round King Neptune, led by the god
Cupid.

Unfortunately the early farm buildings and the temple complex
which replaced them had been ploughed away to their foundations,
and little is known of upper parts of the buildings. Nothing of the villa
is to be seen at Dewlish today, as the site has been filled in and re-
seeded.

THE COUNTRYSIDE

People once used to imagine the Romano-British countryside as some sort of idyllic parkland with a splendid villa glimpsed through the trees every few miles. It is now realised that the big country houses were certainly there, but the majority of the population lived in small farms and villages not unlike those of the nineteenth and twentieth centuries. In fact by the end of the Roman period the population had risen to a level not to be seen again till the Industrial Revolution.

In some areas of fenland in Lincolnshire, aerial photography has shown that the newly settled land maintained small settlements at intervals of less that one kilometre. Nearer Dorset, the route of the M5 was carefully studied in advance of the building of the motorway. As in Lincolnshire Roman settlements were found to exist much more frequently than had been imagined. In many parts of the country which are sparsely inhabited today, such as the chalk downs in Wessex, settlements abounded.

The result is a current estimate of population at the end of the Roman period of over five million, a considerable increase on a probable Iron age population of one million.

What caused this population explosion? Farming methods were to some extent improved by the introduction of Roman technology, though this is one of the most difficult topics to investigate. More importantly there was a large military and civil market for food which encouraged (or rather demanded) an increase in production. Finally, and most significant of all, the *pax Romana*, or Roman peace, meant that many generations lived their lives in peace without regular warfare to reduce their numbers and ruin agriculture.

As the numbers increased, new settlements sprang up and more and more land was taken into cultivation. In the fens of eastern England Roman water engineering made possible the draining and reclamation of large areas of land which were then intensively settled. In Dorset it

At Turnworth in north Dorset a Romano-British farm (centre left) is preserved, with traces of its fields and lanes. The low sun makes these faint banks visible to the aerial camera.

is doubtful whether any substantial tract of land remained unsettled. In fact the supply of timber for fuel and construction work must have been a major problem for the Durotrigian administration.

Settlement in Dorset was enormously varied. There were the villas occupying the choicest positions and some of the best land. There were farms, large and small, of less than villa status. There were hamlets consisting of several farms grouped together. There were small villages and large villages. In fact, a similar variety of settlement existed to that of today with, of course, a much larger percentage of the population living in the country.

The formal changes brought about by the Romans centred mainly on the towns. Only gradually did the effects reach the countryside. A Durotrigian farmer continued to live as his ancestors had; his house was round, built of timber and thatched. His fields were small, the size that could be ploughed in a day. (His fields can still be seen in many places – they are referred to by archaeologists as 'Celtic' fields). He grew spelt (a primitive form of wheat), and kept the usual domesticated animals; sheep, goats, pigs and cattle.

Smacam Down near Cerne Abbas. The whole landscape is covered with the pattern of small fields characteristic of farming in the Iron Age and Roman periods. A small farm lies in the bushes a little right of centre.

Gradually changes came about. The pottery bought in Dorchester changed shape because it was primarily made for the military market. The farmer could buy more of it, as the new towns and the army provided a profitable market for his produce even after taxation.

New crops were introduced, including rye, oats, vetch and flax. In addition there was cabbage, parsnip, turnip, carrot and other vegetables. In favourable areas fruit trees were grown, including the vine, plum, apple, mulberry and walnut. Wine was the Roman drink, but it never entirely replaced beer drinking in Britain. Wine must have been made in Dorset but, as now, found it difficult to compete with wine from more favourable growing areas on the continent.

The farmer's house might have stayed as it was, as round huts are found throughout Roman Britain. But where Roman influence was stronger, houses were gradually rebuilt in Roman style. The critical change was to a rectangular shape; with it came tiled roofs and painted and plastered walls.

The best known Roman village site in Dorset is Meriden Down near Winterbourne Houghton. Like many such villages it lies not in the valley with the later medieval villages, but on a chalk spur on comparatively high ground. It occupies nearly two hectares. Like a deserted medieval village it includes platforms representing ruined houses (some rectangular, some circular), working areas and small enclosures. Interestingly, the houses lie centrally in an area cut off by fences from the surrounding fields. Rather than the houses surrounding the village green, the green surrounds the houses.

But other villages are different, and every imaginable shape occurs, including long streets with houses either side, and houses clustered round what looks almost like a village green. One of the few excavated hamlets is at Studland on Poole Harbour. Here buildings dated from the conquest to the end of the Roman period. Round huts were succeeded on the same sites by roughly rectangular huts measuring about 12 metres by 7 metres. These were still of wattle and daub, but had substantial stone foundations. They were rebuilt many times, but basically were 'longhouses' where the family lived in one end and the animals in the other. This was the form of the original farm buildings at the Dewlish villa site, but there further development took place.

It is often said that life in the countryside changed little from Iron Age times. But this cannot be entirely true within the boundaries of the Roman province. No doubt the Durotrigian farmer grumbled, but he lived at peace most of the time, had a large family, fed them well, sold his produce profitably in the markets and bought himself some of the trappings of Roman civilisation in the form of clothes and ornaments. His house became rectangular, perhaps roofed in tile, distinctly drier and more comfortable. No longer was it necessary to bury the corn in the ground to preserve it, and he learnt (especially if he was close to one of the more Romanised villa estates) to dry his corn in kilns and keep it in granaries.

Some suggestion has been made that the villa estates, especially in the south-west, changed the ancient landscape of Celtic fields and made their profits from large scale sheep farming. Certainly at the Dewlish villa some small fields appear to have been obliterated and open parkland created. But at other villas where environmental evidence shows what farming operations were going on, it is clear that most of the activities of traditional mixed farming were undertaken.

RELIGION

The Roman world had many religions, and for the first three centuries AD any religion was tolerated by government provided it obeyed the rules. This meant that it had to allow for the deity of the emperor, and this presented little if any difficulty to the many gods of the Greek and Roman Pantheon.

Christianity of course could not allow the deity of the emperor, and this led to the persecution of Christians, particularly under the emperors Nero and Diocletian. But Christianity was a very different religion to most of the others.

Following the conversion of the emperor Constantine in 312 AD, Christianity became the official and required faith of the empire. Some of the other religions suffered repression in their turn, but many continued to flourish in far off corners of the empire, and under the emperor Julian there was a revival of the old religions.

THE PANTHEON

Until the spread of Christianity, most Romans (and Greeks before them) worshipped the many and varied gods of the Pantheon. This is difficult for us to understand, since a traditional Roman god was completely unlike any modern idea of God.

The gods (note the plural) were simply a superhuman race, giant in stature, immortal, and living on Mount Olympus or other magical and inaccessible locations. They lived their own lives and obeyed no moral rules in doing so. They fought, stole and went to bed with the wrong partners; Jupiter was their king, and Juno their queen. They all had special attributes, for example Mars, god of war, and Venus, goddess of love and beauty. The gods were not necessarily concerned with human life at all; they just carried on with their own affairs. But, of course, they were all powerful and could if they wished intervene in human life to considerable effect. Thus it was that enormous sums of money were expended both at public and private level to catch the interest of a god and persuade him or her to intervene in human life. This was done by the provision of temples, expensive and attractive buildings, which provide some of the very best examples of classical architecture; the Parthenon in Athens was simply the home provided by the Athenians for their patron goddess Athene.

You hoped that the god would find your temple irresistibly attractive and reside there. The temple was the god's home and no one was allowed in except the priest or priestess. Assemblies of people, if they happened at all, occurred around an outdoor altar in front of the temple. Grand ceremonies were carried out at state level, and at a personal level you attracted the god's attention by making offerings of small cakes, wine, small animals, a bull – the more expensive, the more likely to succeed! Food offerings were consumed by the priests on the god's behalf.

Excavations of temples always produce examples of this process, since the wealthy, when successful, recorded their offerings on stone altars which can still be read. The best instance in the province of Britain is at Bath where Sulis, goddess of the hot spring, was worshipped. In the days of primitive medicine those gods which offered healing were most successful in financial terms; this accounts for the great wealth of the buildings in the temple complex at Bath.

DORSET

When the Romans came to Britain they found many gods being worshipped in a similar way to their own. This presented no problem; the gods carried on, and in many cases were declared to be identical with particular Roman gods. For instance Sulis at Bath was equated with Minerva, and is addressed on some inscriptions by the double name.

The only exception was the religion of the Druids. This, we are told, involved human sacrifice and other unmentionable horrors. Druidism was forbidden and the historian Tacitus gives a graphic description of the violent destruction of the priests and their sacred groves on Anglesey.

A panel from one of the mosaic floors at Frampton
Roman villa shows the god Mars in full armour,
oddly plucking a leaf from a tree.

We do not know if the Druids operated among the Durotriges,
though it is likely enough. But it is almost certain that throughout
Dorset local gods existed in a style very similar to the Roman gods;
and these would have been worshipped at magical spots such as
forests and springs. By the spring at Cerne Abbas is the huge chalk
figure of a fertility god; perhaps in the Cerne Giant we can actually see
a picture of a native Durotrigian god, as assimilated into the Roman
system.

No doubt with Roman names as well as their own, these gods
continued to be worshipped in the countryside. In the towns there will
have been greater pressure for allegiance to be transferred to the
Roman gods themselves. As we shall see, many of these native gods
staged a comeback in the later years of Roman Britain.

Neither in Dorchester nor in Ilchester has a single temple been found to any god, native or Roman, though no doubt they existed. Oddly enough it is the countryside which has given us some very spectacular evidence. In two Dorset villas the mosaic floors of the main reception-cum-dining room (*triclinium*) contain one of the symbols of Christianity. This was the logo formed from the Greek letters *chi* and *rho*, which together represent *chr*, the first letters of Christ's name.

At Frampton villa, 5 miles west of Dorchester in the valley of the Frome, the main pavement featured figures from classical mythology, including Cupid, Neptune, and the story of Bellerophon and the Chimaera. Neptune and Cupid are honoured in lines of verse set into the floor. But oddly the dining apse opening from the main room has on its threshold three floral whorls on either side of a roundel containing the *chi-rho* symbol.

It raises intriguing but unanswerable questions. Was the owner Christian? If so, what is Neptune doing so prominently elsewhere on the floor? Was the side-room used as a Christian chapel and its use symbolised in the floor as you entered? Perhaps Neptune and the other ancient gods were regarded as mere figures of mythology, not seen to be in conflict with Christianity? Nevertheless in several parts of the room pictures of mythological scenes have at some time been hacked from the floor, and this may be the work of Christians who felt they were inappropriate.

At Hinton St Mary near Sturminster Newton, the pictures are less equivocal. Bellerophon and the Chimaera appear in the apse, but the central panel in the main room shows the head and shoulders of a man; behind him is the *chi-rho* symbol, and on either side pomegranates, symbols of eternal life. This picture probably represents Christ. These mosaic floors, taken together with evidence from Dorchester, at least confirm that in the 4th century AD Christianity had come to Dorset, and was probably widespread.

In the cemetery at Poundbury outside Dorchester upwards of 1,000 burials were found, aligned in Christian fashion and the bodies fully extended on their backs. The manner of burial coupled with the absence of grave goods, and the occasional find of a *chi-rho* coin

Hinton St Mary Roman villa. The floor of the dining room, now in the British Museum. Perhaps the most famous Roman mosaic in Britain because of the figure in the centre of the lower part of the floor; this is probably Christ, since the chi-rho symbol lies behind the head, and it is flanked by pomegranates, symbols of eternal life.

pierced for wearing round the neck, indicate that this was one of the burial places of the Christian community in *Durnovaria*. There must have been a church, similar to the small one known from Silchester. Moreover, in the Poundbury cemetery among the graves were several mausolea. In one of these fragments of painted wall decoration show rows of officials with staffs of office, perhaps church elders. The decoration includes one *chi-rho*.

Other finds from Dorset confirm the practice of Christianity. These include two silver rings from the villa at Fifehead Neville with *chi-rho* on the bezel, and a group of silver spoons found at Somerleigh Court in Dorchester. One of these has a fish depicted on the bowl, and another the message *Augustine vivas*, both indicating Christian use. The spoons, found with 50 silver coins, may well have been part of the ritual of the Dorchester church, buried in some emergency and never recovered.

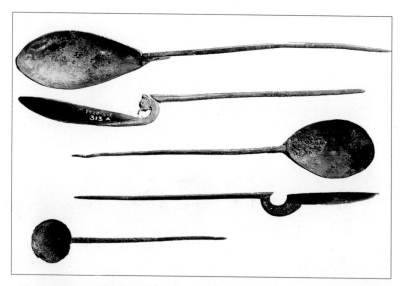

Above Silver spoons found at Somerleigh Court in Dorchester. These may have been used in Christian ritual, as one has a fish drawn in the bowl and another has a Christian inscription.
Opposite page The Cerne Giant. This fertility god, carved on the chalk hillside, probably dates from the Roman period. He may well be a native god equated with the Roman god Hercules.

The major evidence for the revival of pagan religion at the end of the Roman period lies in two Romano-Celtic temples, one at Maiden Castle and the other at Jordan Hill, near Weymouth.

Jordan Hill is much damaged and badly excavated; its identity is not entirely certain. But the Maiden Castle temple was excavated by Wheeler, and a full account can be read in his report on the hillfort. The temple consisted of a square *cella* or shrine, surrounded by a square portico. This was the usual shape in the third and fourth centuries for temples of native gods, as distinct from the classical Roman ones, who are more likely to have had classical temples.

Beside the Maiden Castle temple lay a small two-roomed house, presumably for the priest. There is some evidence that all the eastern end of the hillfort was walled off to form the temple precinct. It seems to have been reasonably prosperous, but we have no means of knowing the name of the god. Most interesting of all is the fact that underneath the ruins of the temple (which can still be seen) Wheeler found a small wooden hut from the hillfort of 400 years before the temple, and this hut may itself have been a shrine. It is possible that one of the gods of the Durotriges worshipped in the old hillfort had retained his identity, to benefit from a pagan revival in the late fourth century.

Certainly there was a pagan revival at this time and one wonders what the Christian community thought of it. In some parts of Britain such temples became extremely prosperous and the best known example is at Lydney in Gloucestershire, also excavated by Wheeler.

At the villa at Dewlish the late fourth century saw the building of a small square temple and an attendant house; this too may have been for a Celtic god, but heavy ploughing has removed any certain evidence.

A recently discovered eight-sided temple enclosure at Badbury Rings has yet to yield up its secrets.

TRADE AND INDUSTRY

One of the attractions which brought the Romans to Britain was the prospect of profits from a variety of industries. The first century geographer Strabo described pre-Roman Britain as exporting gold, silver, iron, slaves, corn, cattle, hides and hunting dogs.

Mines for the various metals were the personal property of the emperor and run for his private profit by procurators. These mines provided some of the few instances in Roman Britain where industry operated on the large, messy scale more familiar to us from the Industrial Revolution. The most famous of these is perhaps the gold mine at Dolaucothi in Central Wales, with its several aqueducts supplying water power. Similar scenes could be found at the lead and silver mines of Charterhouse, the tin mines of Cornwall, the iron mines of the Weald, and other mining centres.

No metal was mined in Dorset, but there were two major and no doubt profitable industries; stone and pottery. The pottery industry was almost certainly in private Durotrigian hands, while the stone industries may have had local or just possibly imperial owners.

POTTERY

In the cemeteries found at Maiden Castle the dead were buried with a variety of pottery bowls to provide food for their journey to another world. These pots included distinctive shallow bowls known to archaeologists as 'war-cemetery' bowls. Along with most of the other pottery found at Maiden Castle, they were made by a thriving prehistoric pottery industry based in Purbeck and using the ballclays and sands from the tertiary deposits north of the chalk ridge. In fact the distribution of this pottery is one of the ways in which the territory of the Durotriges is defined.

The Durotrigian potters made distinctive bowls, plates, cups,

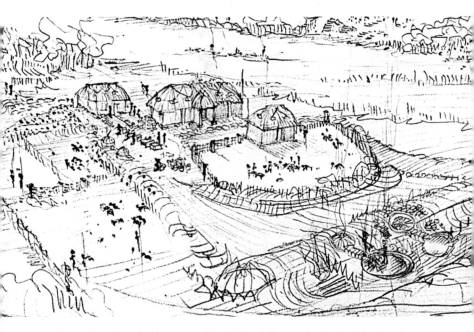

Peter Woodward's drawing of an industrial scene in Purbeck in the Roman period, showing various stages in the production of pottery.

cooking pots and jugs, produced without the aid of a wheel, and finished by burnishing the surface with a bone polisher. The pots were fired in clamps without the use of permanent kilns. Within a year or two of its arrival the Second Legion was using Durotrigian pottery of most types in its camps for cooking purposes. It imported Samian and other fine wares from Gaul for table use.

As the years passed and the army moved on to the Midlands, Wales, and finally the northern frontiers, the Durotrigian potters continued to supply vast quantities of kitchen ware. Other purchases were made of course, but in a typical excavation on Hadrian's Wall, for instance, over half of the coarse pottery found will be from the Durotrigian industry. Many boats must have sailed from Poole harbour laden with the products, on the journey to the Tyne at South Shields and other northern harbours.

At first the traditional Durotrigian shapes were produced. But gradually the potters were influenced by the requirements of their new customers, and new shapes appeared, particularly cooking pots, flange rimmed bowls, and pie dishes. Amazingly the potters did not change their methods of working. They did not change over to using wheels, and they continued for the most part to fire in temporary clamps. Similarly they continued to burnish the pots, with a little token decoration in the form of incised wavy lines. Almost all the pots were intended to be black, and were fired with the air excluded in the final stages, to produce that effect.

Not surprisingly this pottery is known to archaeologists as Black Burnished ware. The proof that the pottery on Hadrian's Wall was identical to that found in Dorchester was one of the early triumphs of the scientific approach to archaeology. It was done at Southampton University by the examination of thin sections of pottery under the microscope; this proved that the minerals present in the pots found in the north could only have come from Purbeck.

'Black-burnished' pottery made in Purbeck in the Roman period.
This was the most successful of the industries of the Durotriges.
From left to right: a flanged bowl or pie dish, a cooking pot and a jug.
These are all on display in Dorset County Museum.

[65]

The stone found in Roman buildings in Dorset came from a variety of quarries. Dressed stone in the Dewlish villa and coffins from the Poundbury cemetery were made of Hamstone from Ham Hill, near Ilminster. Some Chilmark stone appears at Dewlish also. Portland stone is extensively used for buildings and particularly for fourth century coffins on the island. But the most active industry appears to have been in Purbeck, where a variety of stone types were quarried. Limestone from various beds was used for almost every building purpose, from quoins to roof tiles. Thousands of diamond pattern

A Hamstone finial from the roof of the Roman Villa at Dewlish.

A newly opened Hamstone coffin from the Roman Christian cemetery at Poundbury. The body has been covered in gypsum to preserve it.

stone tiles have been found on Roman sites in Dorset.

More specialised was Purbeck Marble. This is a shelly limestone which can be cut and polished to a high degree – it has been used in more recent times, and can be seen in the columns of Salisbury cathedral. All the marble appears to have been quarried away in the Middle Ages, so it is not clear where the quarries were; but one may have been at Wilkswood, near Langton Matravers. It was moved surprising distances in Roman Britain, and has been found as far away as London and Chester. It was mainly used for finely dressed stone, especially inscriptions. The famous inscription from Chichester mentioning the name of Cogidubnus is of Purbeck marble showing that this industry (which does not seem to have existed before the Romans) had developed early in the history of Roman Britain.

No doubt the Roman taste for marble generated a search in likely areas for a substitute. A temple dedication slab at *Verulamium* is made of Purbeck marble, as is the tombstone of Carinus at Dorchester.

One unusual industry was based on Kimmeridge shale. This bituminous shale is found at Kimmeridge Bay and had been worked in

A table or chair leg made of Kimmeridge shale.
Many things were made of this material, from
bangles to panelling for baths.

prehistoric times. It can be burnt as fuel, but more particularly, when
newly quarried, can be worked almost like wood, especially on a
lathe. It was then polished to a high gloss black finish. Its uses
included the manufacture of bangles, beads, plates, dishes, bowls, and
furniture including tables and chairs. There were also decorated trays
and architectural features such as wall panels and mosaic tesserae. The
cold plunge bath at Dewlish villa was lined with slabs of Kimmeridge
shale, and this material too was widely traded across Britain.

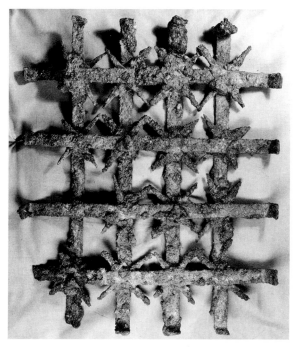

Iron window grill from the Roman villa at Hinton St Mary. This is on view in the British Museum, along with the famous mosaic floor.

OTHER INDUSTRIES

These were the industries which achieved province-wide success. In addition the supply of timber and charcoal was important throughout Dorset, and crystallization of salt from sea water occurred at a number of places along the coast. A whole range of industries were related to farming, including leather working. Cloaks made from British wool were famous as far afield as Rome, and no doubt some came from Dorset.

In the towns there will have been an enormous number of small establishments providing services and products made on the premises, from butchers and greengrocers to metalworkers of every sort. A time traveller to Roman Dorset would find a complex pattern of trade not all that dissimilar to that of the nineteenth and early twentieth century.

THE END OF ROMAN RULE

The popular view of the end of Roman Britain is that a decision was taken in Rome to withdraw, and that the legions which arrived in 43 AD packed their bags and marched to the ports, to the cheers of the assembled people. Reality was very much more complex.

For a start, Britain had been under Roman rule for nearly 400 years, the equivalent of the period from Tudor times to the present day. Britain was unquestionably part of the Roman world and shared in its relative prosperity. The departure of Roman armies was something to be feared, not welcomed, as it left the country exposed to attack from outside the frontiers. In Britain's case the threat came from the Picts of Scotland, the Scots of Ireland, and the Saxons and other groups from northern Europe.

The army itself had changed; no longer were the legions the dominant units. Some still existed (the Second Augustan was at Richborough in a much reduced form) but many were now small infantry regiments. Pride of place was held by cavalry regiments formed to face the attacks of horse-borne barbarians from central Europe.

Even the names of civil and military leaders had changed by the fourth century. The military commander on the frontier was known as the Duke of Britain (*Dux Britanniarum*) and the commander responsible for naval defences in the south-east was the Count of the Saxon Shore (*Comes Litoris Saxonici*). Britain was by now five smaller provinces grouped to form a diocese, and the civilian governor was called the Vicar (*vicarius*).

A major crisis occurred in 367 AD when the Picts, the Scots and the Saxons apparently conspired (or so the Romans thought) to attack Britain at the same time, and the country was overrun. It could easily have been the end of Roman Britain. But somehow the central government, itself under severe pressure from barbarian attacks managed to find the resources to rescue Britain. A senior general, Theodosius, spent two years restoring normality, and putting coastal defences and Hadrian's Wall back in working order.

At this time in Dorset we get the first sign of the end. Where Ackling Dyke passed through the old prehistoric frontier of the tribe's territory at Bokerley Junction, the road was temporarily blocked by an extension of the Iron Age dyke. Soon afterwards it was reopened, but we have a glimpse of the *civitas* of the Durotriges putting their old defences in order to protect themselves from the chaos in other parts of the province. There is not enough evidence to say whether they were successful. There would have been no soldiers in Dorset, but there may have been a town militia to protect Dorchester and Ilchester, and others may have been armed for the occasion in spite of the Roman law which forbade it. Certainly neither towns nor villas show signs of destruction at this date.

Amazingly it is in this very period following the barbarian conspiracy that the towns and villas seem to have reached their greatest prosperity, and this is very difficult to explain, except by an influx of people trying to escape from areas where the trouble was worse. Britain was then reasonably well defended. But between 383 and 407 troops were repeatedly withdrawn from Britain to help on the continent, or to intervene on behalf of British commanders who thought they could make a better job of the western emperorship than the man in command at the time. Magnus Maximus took the troops with him in 383, and left chaos behind. Stilicho restored the situation in 396, only for the adventure to be repeated by Constantine III in 407. At this point Roman control of Britain lapsed, and it becomes very difficult to know what happened in Britain in any detail. The traditional date for the end of Roman Britain is 410; in that year the *civitates* of Britain on their own account wrote to the emperor Honorius, explained their plight and what they were doing to help themselves.

Honorius wrote back and told them to see to their own defence. Clearly by this time (probably in 410 or thereabouts) Roman officials had been withdrawn, the vicar's palace in London was empty, and the civil service left without a job. This is proved by the almost complete absence of coins after this date; no one was being paid in Britain by the Roman government, and so no coins came into the country.

In Dorset Bokerley Dyke was closed and opened several times around the turn of the century as the Durotriges defended themselves. But this is almost the sum total of archaeological evidence from Dorset, apart from the general decay of the towns, villas and the whole economic structure.

The archaeologist's problem at this period is that coins ceased to be circulated and pottery ceased to be made; at a stroke the two main sources of dating evidence disappear.

At some point in the first decade of the fifth century coins of 402 were dropped in fireplaces built on the mosaics of Dewlish Villa; clearly the buildings were in use, but not in the grand style of its former owners. Nevertheless nothing violent happened. The villa had been cleared of all its possessions and the rooms were empty when weather and decay ultimately led to the collapse of the roof.

Life in Dorchester and Ilchester must have gone on, the walls becoming especially significant. Almost certainly a town militia defended them and a Durotrigian army manned the frontier. But the whole complex economic structure was collapsing. No money meant a return to the prehistoric practice of barter. Food and shelter were the important things. The markets for pottery and stone products were inaccessible. The industries collapsed and their owners were no longer wealthy. The materials for repairing buildings were not available, and the goods essential to Roman life unobtainable. The feeling of being shut out of the familiar Roman world must have been depressing indeed.

As the years passed Dorset returned more and more to the pattern of life of its prehistoric past – which had never really disappeared in the countryside anyway. How long the towns survived we cannot yet tell. It must have been well into the fifth century and perhaps even longer.

In the east Saxons and others had been settling for many years already, in some cases by arrangement, in others by force. But they did not reach the south-west in any numbers for another two centuries, and life in Dorset must have gone on.

We have tantalising glimpses of the struggle to keep the Saxons out. We hear of great leaders in Britain heading the resistance; Vortigern,

Bokerley Dyke from the air. This bank and ditch was the pre-Roman
frontier of the Durotriges, and was brought back into use after Roman rule
from London collapsed in the early fifth century.

Ambrosius Aurelianus, and Arthur. Victories were won, including a famous one at Mount Badon, which may have been in Dorset.

At South Cadbury Castle in Somerset, and at other sites in the south west, evidence has recently been found of the old hillforts being reoccupied by these sub-Roman leaders. They can be dated, particularly by the wine jars they were importing from the Mediterranean. No such site has been found in Dorset yet, but a major cemetery belonging to this period was recently found on the line of the Topuddle bypass.

In the end Saxon armies and settlers overran Dorset, probably on a large scale in the early seventh century. After that a new story begins.

PLACES TO VISIT

MAIDEN CASTLE. 2 miles south-west of Dorchester on the A354 (SY 6688). Scene of the assault by the Second Augusta Legion.

HOD HILL. 4 miles north-west of Blandford on the A350 (ST 8510). Roman fort inserted into Iron Age hillfort.

SOUTH CADBURY CASTLE. 10 miles north-east of Yeovil on the A303 (ST 6225). Iron Age hillfort re-occupied in the late Roman period by King Arthur or someone like him.

BADBURY RINGS. 4 miles north-east of Wimborne. Roman road junction beside Iron Age hillfort (ST 966034).

DORCHESTER, MAUMBURY RINGS. Where the Weymouth road crosses the railway (SY 690 899). Roman amphitheatre.

DORCHESTER, CARINUS TOMBSTONE. Original in St George's Church, Fordington (SY 699 905), replica in Dorset County Museum.

DORCHESTER, TOWN WALL. Surviving fragment (SY 689 906) just south of the Top o' Town roundabout.

DORCHESTER, TOWN HOUSE. Displayed behind County Hall (SY 689 909).

DORCHESTER, AQUEDUCT. Follows the Frome valley to the north-west of Dorchester to Frampton. It can best be seen west of Poundbury hillfort and in Fordington Bottom (SY 6791).

DORCHESTER, DORSET COUNTY MUSEUM. In High West Street; contains the major collection of archaeological material from the county including many Roman finds.

PRIEST'S HOUSE MUSEUM, WIMBORNE. Finds from the Tarrant Hinton Roman Villa, including the tombstone, the pump and the painted wall plaster.

ACKLING DYKE, ROMAN ROAD. Join it half a mile south east of Handley roundabout on the A354 from Blandford to Salisbury (where the B3081 crosses – SU 016 164). The road can be followed from here south-west towards Badbury Rings for over 9 miles.

BOKERLEY DYKE, FRONTIER EARTHWORK. The A354 crosses it at Bokerley Junction (SU 033 198), just beyond Woodyates on the way from Blandford to Salisbury.

THORNCOMBE WOOD, ROMAN ROAD. 4 miles east of Dorchester near Higher Bockhampton. The road is visible for over a mile through Thorncombe Wood into Puddletown Forest, starting at SY 726 919.

VILLAS. No Dorset villa is on view to the public. Finds can be seen and inquiries made about excavations in progress at the museums at Dorchester, Poole and Wimborne.

MAIDEN CASTLE, ROMAN TEMPLE. The foundations of the temple (SY 672 885) are on view in the hillfort – see above.

JORDAN HILL, ROMAN TEMPLE. Near Bowleaze Cove, 2 miles east along the coast from Weymouth (SY 699 822). Foundations only to be seen.

INDUSTRY. None of the industrial sites in Dorset are on display. Finds may be seen in the museums mentioned above.

FURTHER READING

Information about Dorset itself appears mainly in the publications of the Dorset Natural History and Archaeological Society, who can be contacted at Dorset County Museum in High West Street, Dorchester, DT1 1XA (01305 262735). Their journal, *The Proceedings of the Dorset Natural History and Archaeological Society* has been published annually for over a hundred years. It contains a wealth of information about excavations and discoveries in Dorset. In addition the Society publishes a monograph series in which major excavation reports appear which are too bulky for the *Proceedings*. The Museum will be happy to send an up-to-date list of its publications on receipt of a stamped and addressed envelope.

The second published source for Dorset archaeology is the inventory of archaeological monuments produced by the Royal Commission on Historical Monuments; Dorset is published in five volumes by HMSO. These volumes are the starting point for all systematic research in the county, but need to be updated from the Sites and Monuments Record, a computerised index of archaeological sites and finds held at County Hall, Dorchester.

There are many general books on Roman Britain which provide the background; among the most important are:

Dark, Ken and Petra, *The Landscape of Roman Britain* (1997)
Frere, S.S., *Britannia* (3rd edition 1987)
Frere, S.S. & St Joseph. J.K.S., *Roman Britain from the Air* (1983)
Henig, Martin, *Religion in Roman Britain* (1984)
Peddie, John, *Invasion, the Roman Conquest of Britain* (1987)
Salway, P., *The Oxford Illustrated History of Roman Britain* (1993)
Wacher, J., *The Towns of Roman Britain* (2nd edition 1995)
Webster, G., *The Roman Imperial Army* (3rd edition 1985)

Journal: *Britannia*, published annually by the Society for Promotion of Roman Studies

Map: Ordnance Survey, Map of Roman Britain, (4th edition 1991)

Some detailed excavation reports are particularly relevant – these include:

Farwell, D.E. and Molleson, T. I., *Poundbury Vol.II: The Cemeteries* (1993)
Green, Christopher Sparey, *Excavations at Poundbury Vol.I: The Settlements* (1987)
Lucas, R.N., *The Romano-British Villa at Halstock, Dorset, Excavations 1967-1985* (1993)
Richmond, I.A.R., *Hod Hill* (1968)
Sharples, N.M., *Maiden Castle, Excavations and Field Survey 1985-6* (1991)
Smith, Roland J.C. and others, *Excavations along the Route of the Dorchester By-pass, Dorset 1986-8* (1997)
Wheeler, R.E.M., *Maiden Castle* (1944)
Woodward, Peter J. and others, *Excavations at Greyhound Yard, Dorchester 1981-4* (1993)

Pamphlets:
Putnam, Bill, *Roman Dorchester* published by Dorset County Council 1999
Putnam, Bill, *The Roman Town House at Dorchester* published by Dorset County Council 2000

For children:
Putnam, Maureen, *The Romans in Dorset Book 1: The Roman Conquest* 1997
Putnam, Maureen, *The Romans in Dorset Book 2: Roman Dorchester* 1998.

ACKNOWLEDGEMENTS

I would like to thank Maureen Putnam for her help in preparing this book, the estate of the late Alan Sorrell for his reconstruction drawing on the frontispiece, John Hodgson for his reconstruction drawing on page 35 (top), and Peter Woodward for his drawings on pages 46 and 64.

Some of the illustrations come from the author's own collection but I would also like to thank the following for allowing the inclusion of illustrations in their possession or for which they hold the copyright: Aerofilms; page 61: Cambridge University Collection, © Crown Copyright; pages 43, 52, 53: Dorset County Museum; pages 4, 12, 13, 15, 18, 19, 29, 34, 35 (bottom), 57, 60, 68, 69: Francesca Radcliffe; page 30: Royal Commission Historical Monuments (England), © Crown Copyright; pages 14, 16, 38, 73: Wessex Archaeology; page 42: W.J. White; page 59.

The

DISCOVER DORSET

Series of Books

A series of paperback books providing informative illustrated
introductions to Dorset's history, culture and way of life.
The following titles have so far been published.

BLACKMORE VALE *Hilary Townsend*

BRIDGES *David McFetrich and Jo Parsons*

CASTLES AND FORTS *Colin Pomeroy* COAST & SEA *Sarah Welton*

CRANBORNE CHASE *Desmond Hawkins*

DOWNS, MEADOWS & PASTURES *Jim White*

DRESS AND TEXTILES *Rachel Worth*

FARMHOUSES AND COTTAGES *Michael Billett*

FARMING *J.H.Bettey* FOLLIES *Jonathan Holt*

FOSSILS *Richard Edmonds* GEOLOGY *Paul Ensom*

THE GEORGIANS *Jo Draper* HEATHLANDS *Lesley Haskins*

THE INDUSTRIAL PAST *Peter Stanier*

ISLE OF PURBECK *Paul Hyland* LEGENDS *Jeremy Harte*

LOST VILLAGES *Linda Viner* MILLS *Peter Stanier*

PORTLAND *Stuart Morris* POTTERY *Penny Copland-Griffiths*

THE PREHISTORIC AGE *Bill Putnam*

RAILWAY STATIONS *Mike Oakley*

REGENCY, RIOT AND REFORM *Jo Draper*

RIVERS & STREAMS *John Wright* THE ROMANS *Bill Putnam*

SAXONS AND VIKINGS *David Hinton*

SHIPWRECKS *Maureen Attwooll* STONE QUARRYING *Jo Thomas*

THE VICTORIANS *Jude James* WOODLANDS *Anne Horsfall*

All the books about Dorset published by The Dovecote Press
are available in bookshops throughout the county,
or in case of difficulty direct from the publishers.
The Dovecote Press Ltd, Stanbridge,
Wimborne, Dorset BH21 4JD
Tel: 01258 840549 www.dovecotepress.com